"My friends are my estate."

— Emily Dickinson

Where would I be without you, my dear friend?

I know that a visit with you can turn my day into sunshine.

Don't forget to wish for…

*Fun times, a little nightlife,
and chocolate.*

Life is full of surprises and you are mine.

A friend like you comes around once in a lifetime.

I knew you and I were meant to be friends…

The day we shared our first phone call.

"A friend might well be reckoned the masterpiece of nature."

— Ralph Waldo Emerson

Just two words…

Best Friends

When I need a pick-me-up…

You're there.

"*Never shall I forget the time I spent with you. Please continue to be my friend, as you will always find me yours.*"

— *Ludwig Van Beethoven*

You can't beat an outing with a friend.

Life is never as good as when it's shared with a friend.

*Old friends who
live far away…*

*Hang on to what
they've got.*

"*Treat your friends as you do your pictures, and place them in their best light.*"

— *Jennie Jerome Churchill*

I need my friends in good times and in bad.

Sometimes the best part of my day is time with a friend.

Our lives are wrapped up in each other's.

The glow of a great day together lasts a long time.

Laughter keeps us young.

*Old friends have their hearts
in the right place.*

"*Friendship improves happiness and abates misery, by the doubling of our joy and the dividing of our grief.*"

— *Cicero*

My good friend…

*K*eep me in your thoughts.

I wish I had more time to relax…

With you.

"*Of all the means to insure happiness throughout the whole of life, by far the most important is the acquisition of friends.*"

— *Epicurus*

*R*emember the good times.

*K*eep me in your thoughts.

There's a dream I have…

*Where we go on vacation
and live it up.*

"*A faithful friend is beyond price, and her value cannot be weighted. A faithful friend is a life-giving medicine.*"

— *The Apocrypha*

We have so much to be thankful for...

Beginning with each other.

"*Misfortune tests the sincerity of friends.*"

~ *Aesop*

Why is it that when a friend is in need…

It feels so good to be there for them?

Don't worry…

I 'll find the time.

Keep your faith in me…

I won't let you down.

"*Keep your friendships in repair.*"

~ *Ralph Waldo Emerson*

Life gives us more than we
can handle some days…

And also gives us a friend
to share it with.

*O*ld friends know what
makes the other tick.

*L*ook for the spirit that brings
us together.

Trust in the ways of friends…

*Our past has shown us
the way.*

"The language of friendship is not words but meanings."

— Henry David Thoreau

© 2004 Havoc Publishing
San Diego, California
U.S.A.

Text by Maureen Webster

ISBN 0-7416-4111-9

www.havocpub.com

Made in China